BASICS

DESIGN AND LIVING

JAN KREBS

BASICS

DESIGN AND LIVING

BIRKHÄUSER – PUBLISHERS FOR ARCHITECTURE
BASEL·BOSTON·BERLIN

CONTENTS

FOREWORD

Dwellings are usually the first design projects to be tackled in architecture courses. Even if would-be architects find their way around this area easily at first because of their own experiences of homes, they have to put their own ideas aside and address the topic of housing through the lens of new concepts. When designing living space, the challenge lies in not starting with oneself and one's own needs, but in having the eventual occupants in mind, as their horizons of experience or values can be very different from the planner's. So dwellings must be endowed with qualities that permit the users to develop in their own space and create lives for themselves according to their own ideas. This does not apply to the general home environment alone: the design of individual living areas and spaces is crucial if the occupants are to feel at home and comfortable. So it is important that architects should make deliberate and intensive efforts to create spatial quality in homes.

The "Basics" series of books aims to present the fundamental points about a new field stage by stage. Instead of compiling an extensive compendium of specialist knowledge, it aims to provide students with explanations that are readily understood and give insight into important questions and parameters of the various fields.

This "Design and Living" volume therefore refrains from providing built examples, which are already exhaustively available. For the same reason, it does not offer idealized or polarized guidelines about how to design living space, as dwellings always gives an individual picture of their user and the prevailing social or even climatic conditions. Instead, "Design and Living" explains fundamental concepts, the way the individual living areas can cohere, and building form variations. The aim is to understand approaches to making rooms, living areas and entire residential units fit together, and to be able to use this knowledge to develop one's own housing construction design work competently and prudently.

This book is intended to help readers to find an easy way into the complex subject of housing design, emphasizing fundamental aspects of living. The chapter Basics presents general conditions and provides examples of design approaches. The chapter Elements of living describes the various uses and functions of a home, along with general and special requirements. Finally, the book examines the fundamentals of approaches to the urban context and their impact on home life, and the fundamentals of access in the chapter Building forms.

Bert Bielefeld, Editor

INTRODUCTION: WHAT IS A HOME?

The term "home" covers a large number of needs and requirements. A home requires different areas, including those for sleeping, cooking, eating and hygiene, in a single location. Home life is something quite ordinary in this context, but by no means unimportant. Life at home is one way people have of defining themselves. The place a person chooses to live identifies their preferences and constraints. The size, form and furnishings of a home, and the way it is occupied, influence the states of mind of the people in it. It is a place for retreat, but also a place for communication; for both introverted and extroverted situations. Fundamentally different sets of events may take place at the same time, and it is not always possible to combine the various interests and functions without making compromises.

Homes are also linked with constantly advancing personal change. This is particularly clear in the way a person develops in our society: childhood – youth – a period of education – a period of working and establishing a family – retirement – old age. These stages in life usually bring different needs with them, and thus changes in the living environment. The home is adapted to the changing life situation as much as possible. Such possibilities are limited. It is often simpler to move than to modify, extend or improve the current home while still living in it. There are homes for all walks of life and in all price classes, but searching for a home is seldom simple. We have fixed ideas about what we want for a home, and make concessions only for financial or time reasons.

Planning a residential unit should not only address the necessary functions and resultant building costs, but also fundamentally aspire to creating a higher quality of living. The occupant's needs are an important basis for the design. If plans are made on an individual basis, if the future occupant is known, his or her ideas can be considered directly and the home is tailor-made. Without a particular user in mind, for example when building rental homes or developing property, the planner has to work on the basis of the general requirements of a fictitious target group. Here it is usual to design the most flexible standard ground plans for different users, leaving sufficient scope for individuality, but also accounting for the housing market and demand in the long term.

There have always been and still are different forms of housing all over the world. Regional developments depend on different climatic conditions, local features such as topography and material resources, and not least the general cultural situation. Thus, parameters in desert regions are different from those in temperate zones, cities have different demands from thinly populated areas, and so the world's many housing cultures are distinct from each other. This certainly means that many dwelling design criteria are site-specific, but some basic ones can be adapted for other places or at least broaden the designer's horizon and release the potential for ideas. The human being is the measure of past, present and future developments. In this context, looking back at the history of housing can offer numerous ideas and tried-and-tested concepts for current planning tasks.

The current situation in society and housing construction is a snapshot, and future developments are difficult to predict. Nevertheless, the use cycle for a residential building can extend over a number of decades. So we are not building for today's needs alone, but for future generations as well. Aesthetics are less decisive than the substantial quality of the buildings, their functionality and the possibility of varied uses in future. The needs and requirements of a particular society form the basis for housing appropriate to its times. This basis should be constantly examined to create a quality of housing that can persist for as long as possible.

There can be no full answer to the question posed at the outset, "What is a home?" as each person has his or her constantly changing ideas about the subject of home and housing, in addition to general requirements. For this reason, interested readers are invited to ask themselves what a home means, in order to develop their own concepts and find innovative approaches. The following chapters are intended to contribute to this.

BASICS

Housing design creates sequences of events in life that are influenced by a large number of factors inside and outside the home. Important standards for comparison in this context are a person's basic requirements, the dwelling's particular surroundings, and not least the principles of the design approach. These essential considerations for every residential unit are summarized below.

LIFE CYCLES

Human life cycles

Many of the demands made on a home are influenced by the life cycle of human beings, who have changing needs and requirements as they age. If a dwelling's structure cannot be adapted to a new life situation, it could stop being viable, and the occupant will have to look for an appropriate alternative. It therefore makes sense to consider the various phases of life at the preliminary planning stage. An ideal home would be suitable for children, elderly people and disabled people, but of course not all these requirements can be met at the same time, nor do they need to be. For example, cost prevents having a lift in every building with more than one floor. But a number of realistic measures can be implemented sensibly, or at least prepared: for example, service equipment such as switches, power points, and door and window handles can be installed at a level that wheelchair users and children can also reach. Provision can also be made in advance for the necessary space that would allow modification of the home for elderly or disabled people. Features such as unnecessary height differences on a particular floor or very narrow doorways should be checked at the design stage, as aesthetic approaches can clash with later adaptations to a different life situation.

Barrier-free housing

Freedom from barriers is a particular condition for humane dwellings. Barrier-free construction is intended to make it possible for everyone to use a place or a building, regardless of their constitution. Restricted physical capacity should not mean that people are excluded. In this context, special barrier-free homes must be usable by everyone, and put their occupants in a position to live largely independently. People who are blind or who have mobility impairments, people with other disabilities, elderly people, and children benefit in particular. Not every home can and must be barrier-free in this sense, but options for possible modification can be left open.

〉🛈

The building as a whole should also be seen in the context of life or use cycles: most residential buildings are used over periods of several decades, and are refurbished or converted at intervals so that there is no substantial loss of quality, and adaptations are made to changing needs. If these use cycles and the resultant periods of time can be made to match the occupants' life cycles, there are opportunities at the planning stage for measures that can be implemented sensibly during later use. In this way, the changing needs of the occupants can be planned for, not just with respect to long-term economic factors, but also to meet changing needs and necessary modifications.

ORIENTATION

One key quality criterion for a home is natural light. Large or small apertures for admitting light to a home make a considerable difference, and whether the light comes from north, south, east or west is another important factor. The energy plan for a building is also affected by the relative position of the sun. Solar energy is deliberately directed into rooms through windows according to the season and the climate zone, or blocked by sunshading devices to avoid overheating and dazzle. Tree and plant growth, sunshading installations, balconies and protruding roofs can be used for the latter purpose. But small windows or no windows at all may be sensible solutions under certain circumstances; the same applies to the opposite climatic conditions in cold regions, where a great deal of heat energy is lost through the windows on the north side of a building.

Local features such as buildings, roads and open spaces, as well as special topographical features and trees, influence the design for a dwelling

---

\\ Hint:
International and national standards contain instructions for designing barrier-free homes:
ISO/T 9257 Building construction: handicapped people's needs in buildings – design guidelines

There are very few international and national standards relating directly to the creative design of residential buildings. For example, the Swiss standards (SN) contain no regulations of this kind, and other nations produce few standards, with the exception of provisions on function and safety. However, standards are subject to constant change, and international standards, in the guise of ISO (International Organization for Standardization) and EN (Euronorm) are working towards uniformity. Such standards, if they exist at all, represent only part of the necessary planning principles that can influence a housing design. Instruments such as local building regulations are similarly important, along with specific qualities of the materials intended to be used for realization, and not least the future user's requirements.

and determine the orientation of areas for different uses within a ground plan. › see chapter Basics, Areas for different uses Thus, for example, noise from busy roads, or being too overlooked by neighbouring buildings, can be prevented at the design stage by using ancillary rooms to screen off sensitive areas or by minimizing façade apertures appropriately. In contrast, particular views and quiet or protected outdoor areas offer the possibility of opening up the façade deliberately to include the outside space in the design for the interior.

Use times

The principal use times and fundamental lighting requirements of the various usable areas in a home can be determined by relating the rooms to the path of the sun. › see Fig. 1 In this way, the orientation of the building can create areas that will be lit in different ways, and that will take account of the various demands on utilization. › see chapter Basics, Areas for different uses

› 🄸

Points of the
compass

A clear east-west or north-south orientation for a building is favourable in this context, but intermediate solutions may produce good results if the rooms are oriented carefully.

The north side is characterized by little sun and even light. Planners can place the entrance here, or storage and ancillary spaces, as they generally need little light. The sun rises in the east, and when it is low in the sky it will provide sunlight for areas that are used particularly in the morning. This is a good position for kitchens, adults' bedrooms and bathrooms. The south side receives the greatest proportion of sunlight. Areas for children and dining, terraces and conservatories, and other areas that are used particularly from the late morning through to the afternoon benefit most. The sun sets in the west, and can light areas that

🄸

\\ Hint:
For an observer in the northern hemisphere,
all heavenly bodies rise in the east, reach
their highest point in the south and set in
the west. In the southern hemisphere, these
conditions are reversed: the bodies still rise
in the east and set in the west, but reach
their highest point in the north. Thus, the
orientation information applies only to the
northern hemisphere, and must be switched for
the southern hemisphere.

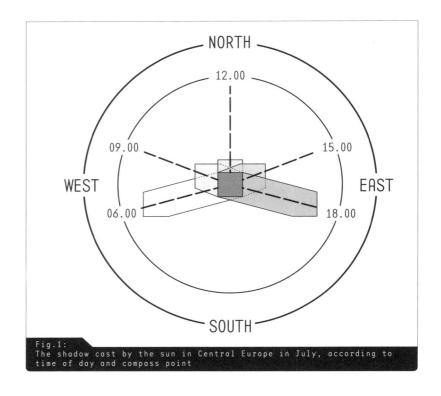

Fig.1:
The shadow cast by the sun in Central Europe in July, according to time of day and compass point

are used particularly in the afternoon and evening, such as general living and leisure areas.

AREAS FOR DIFFERENT USES

A home allocates use areas for everyday events, and these structure the ground plan.

Living areas

Living areas should be equipped so that they are appealing places in which to spend time. The way they are used is greatly influenced by individual needs and the rhythm of the occupants' lives. The needs include living rooms and bedrooms, and comparable areas in a home that can be used individually. > see chapter Elements of living

Functional areas

Functional areas such as the kitchen, bathroom and, where applicable, special working areas, already have their use fixed. They need a

14

particular infrastructure for water supply and drainage, and their use can only be changed by elaborate interventions into the structure of the building. It is the functional areas that first make a set of rooms into a dwelling, and enable the occupants to be largely independent of the outside world. › see chapter Elements of living

Circulation areas

Internal circulation areas, such as corridors, halls and stairs, separate and connect the different areas of a home. The arrangement and design of the circulation areas considerably affects the quality of living, as they determine the sequence of rooms in a home and can impose a hierarchy on transitions. According to the design approach, they may have spatial qualities in addition to their access function, and be used temporarily or permanently. › see chapter Elements of living, Circulation areas

ZONING

The areas for different use in a home described above – the living, function and circulation areas – are interdependent and interwoven within a use matrix. A dwelling can be structured into zones in which different use areas join to form a unit. Thus, for example, intimate areas such as bedrooms and bathroom, possibly combined with an anteroom, can be combined to create such a unit. › see Fig. 2 The spatial structure of kitchen, dining and living room can also join to produce a zone that has a more general character within the home. › see Fig. 3

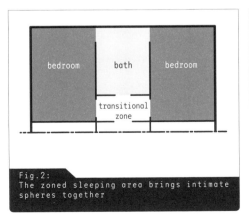

Fig.2:
The zoned sleeping area brings intimate spheres together

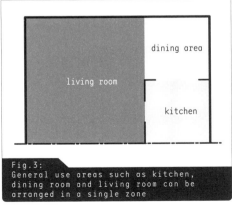

Fig.3:
General use areas such as kitchen, dining room and living room can be arranged in a single zone

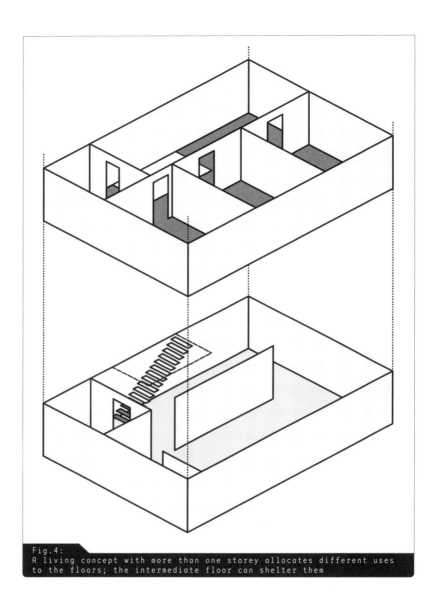

Fig.4:
A living concept with more than one storey allocates different uses to the floors; the intermediate floor can shelter them

If a great deal of space and very different use areas are needed, designing a ground plan on one level can be difficult, as constraints in access and lighting emerge, and the building outline cannot often be freely chosen. A design for living on more than one storey can structure the various use areas on horizontal levels, and thus divide them according to their

Table 1: Specimen criteria for zoning a home		
General area	↔	Private area
Working area	↔	Leisure area
Living area	↔	Function area
Circulation area	↔	Living area
Adults	↔	Children
Link with outdoors	↔	Link with indoors
Vertical links	↔	Horizontal links
Extroverted	↔	Introverted
Open	↔	Closed
Noisy	↔	Quiet
Light	↔	Dark
Day	↔	Night

different uses. › see Fig. 4 For example, an entrance level offers space for more general uses, while rooms for private use are placed on a different floor, and thus screened off spatially by the intermediate floor. Single-family homes, as well as apartments in multi-storey houses, can include two or more floors, allocated to the different use areas. › see chapters Basics, Creating space, and Building forms

Criteria   Possible criteria for zoning a dwelling can also be periods of use, the need for a special work area, and thematic links defined by the occupant's needs. Allocation to the various categories can help to order the related quality or contrasts in use demands within the home. Thus, qualities like noisy/quiet, open/closed and introverted/extroverted are used to develop connections and match them to each other. › see Table 1

CREATING SPACE

The architectural design creates areas and volumes. Adding in the different use areas creates two- and three-dimensional connections, permitting visual links, perspective spatial impressions and communication possibilities. The rooms in a home are defined by ground plan form and volume. Length, width and height can be matched to a number of individual needs and spatial relationships. A particular room can be allocated a specially adapted area and an appropriate volume. In contrast, rooms can be treated use-neutrally and with equal value, so that differences in size do not impose a hierarchy. Another design approach can divide a coherent area or a complete volume into different areas. These different design approaches can be applied throughout a home or can characterize different areas.

> $\mathcal{P}$

Flexibility

In the context of housing construction, flexibility describes the possibility of making individual rooms or a whole residential unit adaptable. The above-mentioned use-neutral room concepts and the open ground plans described below offer starting points for being flexible when changing and adapting rooms while they are in use.

> 🮥

Purpose-built rooms

If rooms are intended only for a designated use, they are purpose-built. Here, the area, scale and connections with other rooms are fixed under consideration of use-specific qualities. > see Fig. 5 The following specifications are customary in detached house building: the living room is usually the largest room, followed by the parents' bedroom, children's bedrooms and the functional areas including kitchen, hygiene and ancillary rooms. In a case like this it is not easy to reallocate room uses if the occupants' ideas change, and it is often impossible to divide the space up differently without a lot of expense. Normally the entire concept of a detached house is directed to the needs and wishes of people, with no long-term change to the home's structure intended.

Use-neutral rooms

If rooms are largely identical in their situation, size and shape, they are use-neutral. This approach makes sense for rented accommodation, for example, which is definitely intended to be used by different occupants over the course of time, as it is not possible to anticipate all the needs of future occupants or changing uses. The rooms are not structured hierarchically, and are interchangeable in terms of use. > see Fig. 6 One of the things this approach explains is the popularity of refurbished homes dating from

$\mathcal{P}$

\\ Example:
The architect Adolf Loos's "Raumplan" (Spatial plan) concept deals with various rooms strictly according to use, area and volume. The ground plan shows a marked independence among the rooms, but as an overall concept them seem like a coherent spatial structure; Müller House in Prague, 1930.

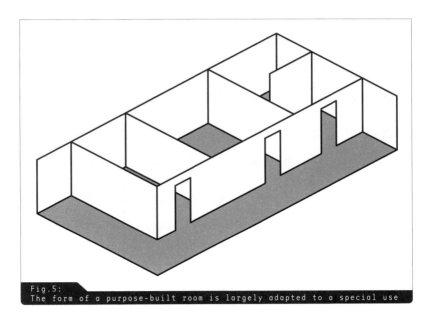

Fig.5:
The form of a purpose-built room is largely adapted to a special use

the early 1870s in Europe, which often have use-neutral ground plans. So if necessary the internal arrangement relating to use can be redefined largely without spatial constraints. It is not just individuals and families who benefit from a home structure of this kind. It is now not just students, but also increasingly professional and elderly people, who share houses and therefore like this kind of flexibility.

\\ Hint:

Flexible ground plans that can be divided up freely and are not limited by statical constraints can be formed structurally by using a free-spanning loadbearing structure: in this case, the ceiling loads are dispersed only via the outer walls or by columns, and all the interior divisions are formed by non-loadbearing walls that can be moved easily. The division and boundaries of rooms can then be determined by the occupant.

But experience shows that homes are seldom adapted on a large scale during use: occupants prefer to move house if need be. So such construction approaches can also lead to higher costs according to the size of the residential unit. Economical crosswall constructions are often used for terraced housing, so that the spaces in between can be used freely (see chapter Building forms, section on terraced housing).

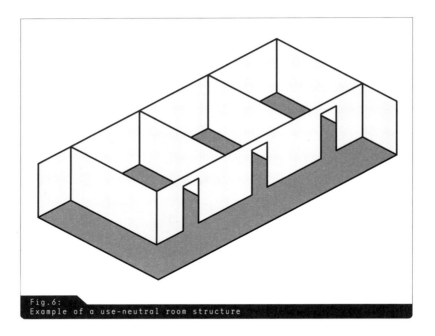

Fig.6:
Example of a use-neutral room structure

Open ground plans combine various uses within a home, within a set of fluent transitions. This design approach creates generously coherent spatial volumes that are not divided by intricate access structures and intermediate walls. Smaller houses and apartments benefit, not least because space is not used for access alone. The clearly delimited spaces created by other dwelling forms are replaced by zoning in an open ground plan, and the zones can be accentuated by changes of material or colour, or of natural light and artificial illumination. › see chapter Basics, Zoning In addition, the open ground plan can be differentiated individually using temporary or (semi-)closed room dividers in the form of open shelf units, (transparent) sliding doors and screens, and thus allow changing spatial impressions and sightlines.

The bathroom and WC are the only functional areas that require a minimum of fixing and isolation, but particular design approaches can blur the boundaries here as well. For example, they can be brought together in a core and positioned centrally in the ground plan. This arrangement produces structurally zoned spaces within a larger area, to accommodate different use areas. › see Fig. 7

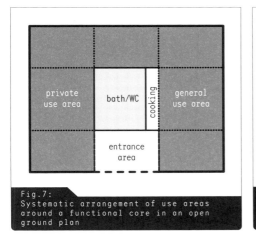

Fig.7:
Systematic arrangement of use areas around a functional core in an open ground plan

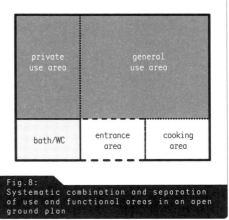

Fig.8:
Systematic combination and separation of use and functional areas in an open ground plan

In addition, private and general living areas can be combined with a kitchen and dining area to give a manageable and generous impression of space. However, in this case an entrance area should be created as a transition from outdoors to indoors, so that the living area is not entered immediately from the outside. › see Fig. 8

Free division makes the open ground plan very flexible for use, and it can deal with many different demands and needs. The single-person household, which is occurring ever more frequently, as well as couples and, temporarily, young families, find this structure appealing. An open ground plan is suitable only to a limited extent for a larger number of occupants with different requirements, as noise and overlapping uses can be disturbing.

Proportions and room height

The height of a room is perceived subjectively and is linked with its ground area. The more open and larger a room is in area, the lower its height will seem to be. › see Fig. 9

Selected use areas can be enhanced by greater room height, especially if they are to be emphasized within the general living concept. So it is possible to accentuate individually important areas, e.g. the living room or dining area, by means of special spatial qualities, and to design other areas of the home more reticently and less voluminously where necessary. › see Fig. 10

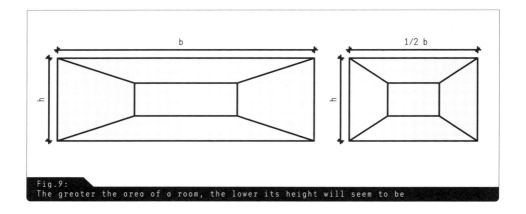

Fig.9:
The greater the area of a room, the lower its height will seem to be

Different
levels in a
room volume
Rooms may also be high enough to be divided into two levels within a single volume. For example, a sleeping area can be fitted with a gallery, or a higher retreat zone can be created in a generally used living area. › see Fig. 11

Planners do not always have the design freedom to choose storey heights for homes in terms of spatial considerations alone, as larger volumes make for additional construction and heating costs. Restrictions to the overall height of a building, in multi-storey housing construction, for example, can restrict design freedom with respect to the room height of individual floors.

Homes with more
than one floor
In residential units with more than one floor, two or more floors can be combined spatially as well as functionally to create special and changing spatial impressions. The necessary vertical access is then differentiated by means of open or closed stairs, which can downplay or intensify the horizontal separation of the floors. It is not just the necessary staircases that offer possible connections: air spaces can present spatial volumes in parts of selected areas. Galleries, often linked to the lower storey by additional stairs, permit direct communication between the floors. › see Fig. 12

Maisonettes
In multi-storey housing construction, the forms produced are called maisonettes – a little house within a larger housing complex. › see Fig. 13 Such homes in particular can be given special spatial qualities by galleries and air spaces.

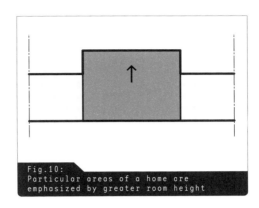

Fig.10:
Particular areas of a home are
emphasized by greater room height

Fig.11:
A gallery creates a second level within
a room volume

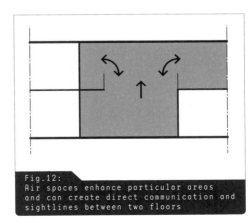

Fig.12:
Air spaces enhance particular areas
and can create direct communication and
sightlines between two floors

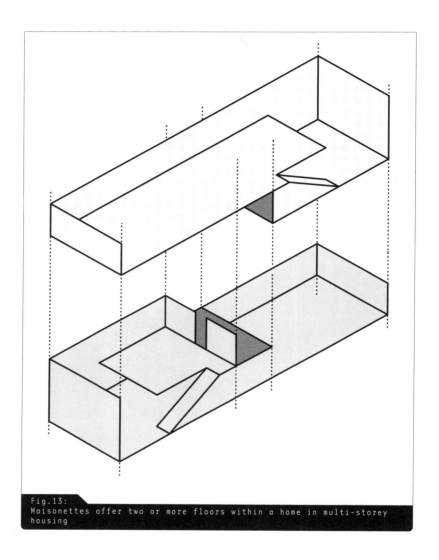

Fig.13:
Maisonettes offer two or more floors within a home in multi-storey housing

Split-level homes

Split-level homes are a particular form of the maisonette. › see Fig. 14 Here, life is conducted on various levels, occupying only one part of the building depth available, and linked by internal stairs. This arrangement means that even comparatively small homes can be zoned on various levels. › see chapter Basics, Zoning

Linking use areas

The transitions from one use area to another may have different design characteristics and thus create spatial accents. Fluent transitions

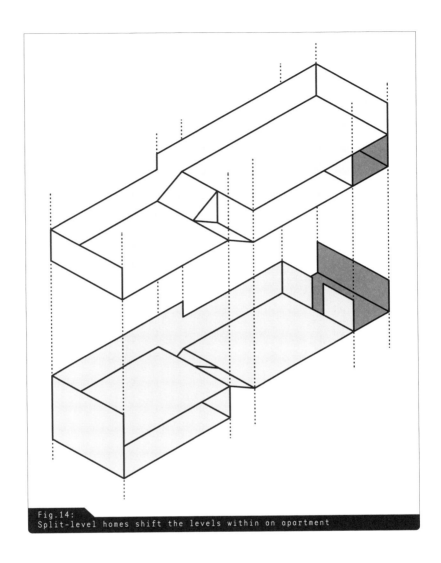

Fig.14:
Split-level homes shift the levels within an apartment

without fixed limits permit largely open perspectives and create a coherent spatial concept. In contrast, structures that form walls divide the various uses and define the different areas clearly. The connecting apertures between the areas influence the effects of the changing space. The width of an aperture is just as important in this context as its height. For example, rather than have a relatively low door, it is possible to create a floor-to-ceiling opening in a wall. A narrow aperture also makes a different effect from a lavish gateway. The individual access points impose a hierarchy on

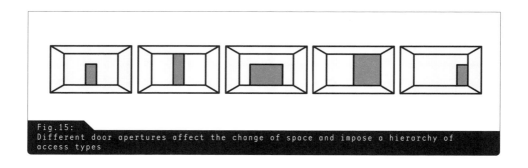

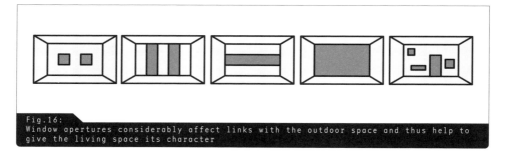

the use areas and express introversion or extroversion. › see Fig. 15 Sliding and hinged doors make it possible to handle divisions or connections flexibly.

Wall apertures do not have to be used exclusively to provide access to use areas. It is possible to use perforations that also simply create visual connections with other rooms, or that can be used functionally as hatches. Circulation areas do not serve their purpose alone either, but can emphasize a change of area and define a spatial transition.

Links with
outdoors

Outdoor space is an important factor for the spatial concept as a whole in this context. Window apertures create visual links with particular local features, thus making their mark on the interior. › see Fig. 16 The perspective is changed by an increase in the height level of a storey. A ground-floor apartment may have the advantage of access at ground level and/or a connection with the garden, but it can also mean that the home is undesirably overlooked from the outside. Measures should be taken where necessary to ensure privacy. The higher the floor level of a home is, the further the eye can roam, and the living space is all the more protected from being overlooked.

›✎

Exits, balconies and terraces combine outdoor and indoor areas; outside areas can become part of the living space. Such a link can be emphasized by space-defining structures in the form of extended walls and pergolas, as well as the use of uniform materials.

\\ Tip:
If the area outside a ground floor apartment is very busy, the risk of being seen can be reduced by a few centimetres' difference in level, combined with an appropriate window sill.

ELEMENTS OF LIVING

The living, function and circulation areas mentioned above are key elements of housing construction design. › see chapter Basics, Areas for different uses These areas can be differentiated with regard to individual needs and general requirements to form the different elements of a dwelling.

SLEEPING

Uses and functions

Sleeping is a basic human need. The quality of one's surroundings affects sleep significantly. This special environment must take very different requirements into account and can be characterized by various conceptual approaches. The bedroom area is principally devoted to the individual phases of rest and recovery, and can be defined by considering these criteria exclusively. This means that the bedroom area is monofunctional and clearly separated from other use areas.

But it is also possible to create potential over and above the principal use and allocate other uses within the sleeping area. It then becomes a general location for the intimate sphere and private purposes according to the time of day.

Various access links are created if other necessary use areas are added. › see Fig. 17 If a dressing room is to be provided, it is an advantage for it to be linked directly with the bedroom, as privacy is destroyed by having to pass through an intermediate corridor. Walk-in wardrobes can be a space-saving and sensible alternative. It also makes sense to be close to the bathroom, to avoid passing through areas that may be used communally. Ideally, direct access should be planned, without a detour via an intermediate corridor.

For reasons of noise insulation, the sleeping area should be screened from rooms that are used communally. If horizontal zoning on different floors is not possible, direct access through "noisy" areas can be avoided by adding in transitional zones. › see chapter Basics, Zoning This recommendation does not necessarily apply to a single-person household, as the uses here are tailored to the daily rhythms of one individual, and internal disturbances by other people are not usually anticipated.

Introverted sleeping areas

Sleeping areas can be matched to individual needs by various design approaches. A bedroom that is almost closed off from the inside and outside worlds, and used exclusively for sleeping, can thus represent the most

29

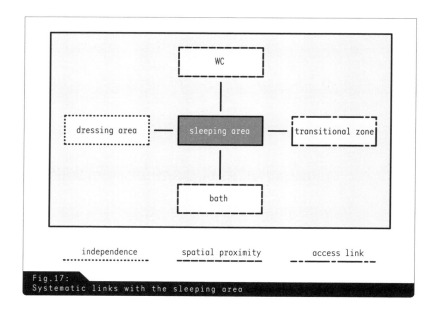

independence   spatial proximity   access link

....   ————————   —·—·——·—

Fig.17:
Systematic links with the sleeping area

extreme form of introverted sleeping area. › see Fig. 18 left External influences that could disturb restful sleep are thus excluded in the planning. Reticent access apertures can underline the room's function as a screened-off area of retreat. Variations in size and proportions create an impression of generous space, or even ascetically functional aspects, if they – as a radical example – are modelled on a ship's bunk.

Sleeping areas relating to the outside   Including the outside area can downplay this introverted quality. A well-placed window or large glazed area, taking orientation into account, changes the light situation considerably and can create special spatial conditions. › see chapter Basics, Orientation In this way, window apertures can provide a source of indirect light and scarcely offer any view out at all. Special window shapes can frame a perspective on the outside world if the viewer is in a particular position, such as lying on the bed. Taking the idea further, in a suitably private situation, the whole outer façade of the bedroom area can be made up of glass elements, which largely cancels out the border between inside and outside. › see Fig. 18 centre left and centre right

Sleeping areas with integrative uses   The bedrooms can also be designed more openly to accommodate other function and use areas, according to access and requirements. For

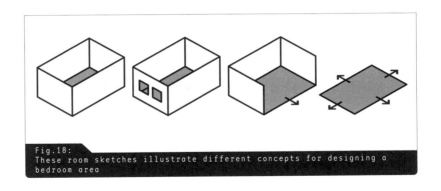

Fig.18:
These room sketches illustrate different concepts for designing a bedroom area

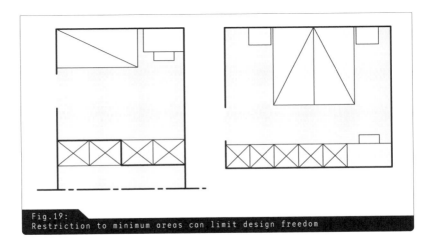

Fig.19:
Restriction to minimum areas can limit design freedom

example, individual areas used for work or leisure can be combined with the sleeping area because these activities take place at different times. › see Fig. 18 centre right

In its most extroverted form, the sleeping area can be placed within an open ground plan and be little different from the other functions and uses in the home. › see Fig. 18 right, and chapter Creating space

Furnishing   Like every use area, the bedroom fundamentally needs sufficient space for furniture, fittings and circulation. › see Fig. 19

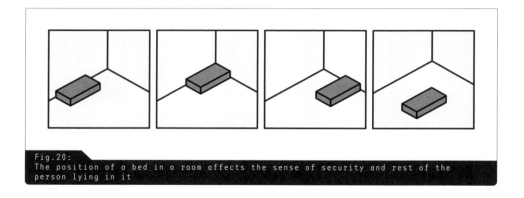

Fig.20:
The position of a bed in a room affects the sense of security and rest of the person lying in it

The smaller the dimensions of these spaces, the more alternative design is limited. Optimizing areas is certainly a desirable planning feature, but it should impede flexibility only to a limited extent, and should permit variable design approaches in terms of subsequent use as well. For example, there are standard-size beds that define how much space is needed. But intermediate sizes, self-built variants, four-poster and raised beds are all places to sleep that do not have to come in standard sizes and may be part of an individual sleeping area.

>

Positioning the bed

Positioning the bed in a room affects conscious and subconscious perceptions. If the bed is in a corner, the whole room and its openings can be in sight, suggesting clarity and security. If the bed is placed centrally, and is also given focus by the position of room apertures and the position of other furnishings, it can be a special centre. > see Fig. 20

\\ Hint:
The length of an individual bed can be worked out by adding approx. 25 cm to the height of the person concerned. Room to move around the bed should be planned to guarantee accessibility. Generally speaking, areas for one person to move in should not be less than 70 cm.

The sleeping area is often also the place where clothes are changed, and therefore needs working space for dressing and the items of clothing involved. › see chapter Elements of living, Storage If there are no plans for a separate dressing room, space should be left for a wardrobe. Care should be taken that there is enough room to move around it, and that it does not stand side on to the door axis and thus hinder access to the room. Built-in floor-to-ceiling cupboards may be an alternative, as they use the space available in the best possible way. However, this does tie up areas and sections of wall, and could possibly constrain other, later design approaches.

EATING

Few social activities have been cultivated traditionally to such an extent as eating. It is celebrated at political and cultural events, typical local dishes define regional and national self-awareness, and special events culminate in a festive meal at home or in a restaurant with our circle of family and friends. It is all the more remarkable that little time is often allowed for everyday breakfasts, lunches or dinners, as work and active leisure are given priority. The status of an eating area in a home thus depends on individual requirements. The number of occupants is important, as well as individual eating habits, and the space available. The eating area also plays a part beyond its actual function as a daily meeting point for the occupants, and for social gatherings. Compact, functional or spacious eating areas are thus designed to suit demands and requirements.

The eating area is usually served by the kitchen and should therefore be placed close to it. Long distances make it more difficult to present food and clear dirty dishes away. If the eating area is outside the kitchen, the working processes can be optimized by a hatch with a space to put things on in front of it. Proximity to the front door and cloakroom should also be taken into account, so that guests can find they way to the laid table or the WC without detours. › see Fig. 21

A clearly delineated space can be allocated to the eating area, thus emphasizing its significance within the home, and its independent and self-contained function. If the room is also to be used for larger gatherings of family or friends, for example, the appropriate space must be planned. Alternatively, the eating area can be placed in a general living area in an all-embracing open living concept. › see chapter Basics, Creating space A constellation of this kind draws no definite borders, and combining areas and functions creates extensive visual links and an impression of generous space. Another advantage is flexible use, as the table can be extended if necessary without constraints on space. If the eating area is to be emphasized in an

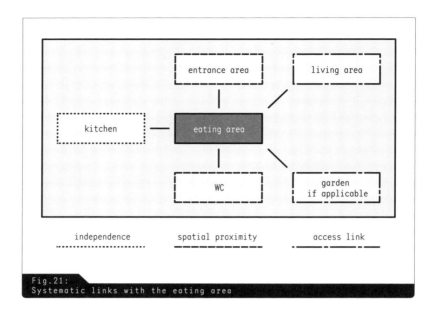

Fig.21:
Systematic links with the eating area

open spatial situation, the obvious thing to do would be to pick up links within the space, and to use varieties of material and lighting creatively.

Eating in the kitchen

Another possibility is to integrate a dining area within a kitchen that also serves as part of the living area. › see chapter Elements of living, Cooking This approach lessens distances to be covered and also enables communication between areas for eating and for preparing food. It is also conceivable in principle to have two eating areas in a home, making a distinction between a functional area for snacks and breakfast in the kitchen and another area elsewhere for the main meals. › see Fig. 22

Links with the outside area

Links with the space outside a home can fundamentally influence the quality of the eating area. Windows coming down to ground level, exits or (roof) terraces can make the outdoor space a conceptual part of the indoor one. The light available and the position in relation to the sun also affect the room, and will help to shape the design, taking the different times of day into consideration. › see chapter Basics, Orientation

Furniture

The arrangement of the furniture and the amount of space needed for furnishing an eating area depend on the spatial concept and the number of users.

›

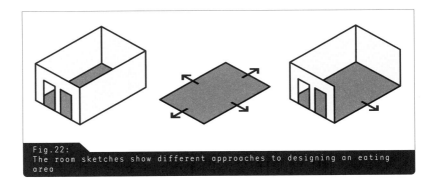

Fig.22:
The room sketches show different approaches to designing an eating area

Dining tables can be placed in various different ways and in a variety of spatial situations. Round tables make it possible for places to be laid equally, while rectangular tables demand a directed arrangement. A freestanding table becomes the dominant element and establishes the key links in the spatial structure. In a corner situation, possibly combined with a corner bench, the eating area will look more essentially functional. Work surfaces can also be used temporarily for a compact snack area inside a kitchen. › see Fig. 23

Uses and functions

WORKING

Work has an important part to play in our everyday life. It determines our rhythm of life, our environment and our social position in society. Our home situation is also influenced by work activity – materially, because

\\ Hint:
One person needs a space at table at least 40 cm deep and 65 cm wide to be able to eat without getting in the way of neighbours. A rectangular dining table for six people will be at least approx. 80–90 cm wide and approx. 180–200 cm long, and the round variant will have a diameter of approx. 125 cm (formula: place width in cm x number of people / 314). If the table is freestanding in the room, the clearance between it and the nearest wall should be at least 1 m, so that it is possible to pass people who are already sitting down.

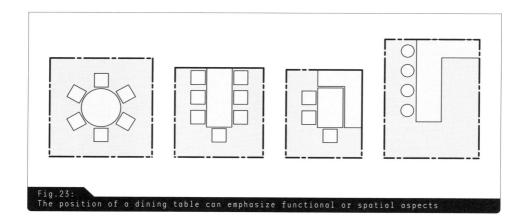

Fig.23:
The position of a dining table can emphasize functional or spatial aspects

it often determines the amount of money available, but also functionally, as various work activities make special demands on a home. Almost every home offers some facilities for brainwork. Communications and computer technology in particularly, with mobile phones, laptop and the Internet, make it possible to work almost anywhere. Thus the bedroom, the dining table or the living-room sofa become temporary workplaces.

But it is often not possible to guarantee an ergonomic, long-term workplace in locations of this kind for various reasons. Lighting conditions, noises and overlapping uses in particular may necessitate having a special home working area if work is to be done regularly.

Room concepts   Designing a working area and creating a sensible categorization and separation in the home depend on requirements, and these are defined by the work involved. Classical office activities like book-keeping, for example, can usually be pursued in a small space, provided that it is designed functionally. For example, if a working area of this kind is placed near the entrance to the home, it is possible to create an independent area for receiving work-related visitors without involving private areas of the home. But as the need arises, the working area may also run into other use areas in an open ground plan. › see chapter Basics, Creating space A number of professions can be pursued at home, shaping and differentiating it through the activity's particular demands. For example, a painter's studio, a sculptor's workshop, a sound studio or a musician's practice room, or even a teacher's study create particular emphases that can scarcely be detached from other use areas and also permit interaction between work and leisure. Here, zoning can suggest helpful approaches for achieving good solutions. › see chapter Basics, Zoning Any links with the outside world that might be needed, lighting and other special criteria such as sound insulation depend on the particular demands of the activity pursued.

RECREATION AND LEISURE

Uses and functions

Many leisure activities take place in an enclosed space, and space is generally provided for recreation and relaxation in the home. A bed is not used exclusively for sleeping, the dining table can also be used for games, the bathtub can be a place for relaxation, and a living room with television and reading area is almost taken for granted as a component of many homes. Often very little intervention is needed to make every room in the home a place with potential for recreation and leisure.

Room concepts

The living area can be central to life in the home and to eating, and is often also used for recreation in the course of everyday leisure. › see Fig. 24

The living room is usually an extrovert part of the home, a central area for spending time, the qualities of which can be enjoyed by guests as well as the occupants. But there are also introverted room concepts that can make the living room into a private area of the home, screened-off inside and outside.

A large living area conveys a generous impression of space and can also be subdivided, for example into reading and play zones, and spaces for communication and multimedia use. › see Fig. 25

A recreation area can be designed with special spatial qualities, e.g. with greater height, or in some cases linked with other uses through air spaces and galleries. › see chapter Basics, Creating space Such expansive planning approaches cannot always be realized, and small and compact living spaces can also be handled in such a way as to create a high-quality area in which to spend time, particularly emphasizing the manageable and comfortable aspects of living. There is also the possibility of adding spaces for other main uses, e.g. eating area and kitchen, to a (small) living room and thus implementing the spatial concept of an open ground plan with various zones. › see chapter Basics, Zoning

Fitness areas, a music room, a library, or other individual leisure areas leave a great deal of scope in the design for creative and integrative solutions. Whether the use is planned to be temporary or long-term will

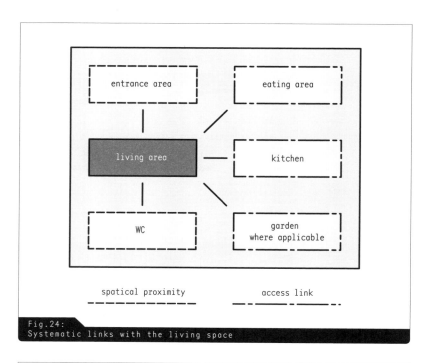

entrance area

eating area

living area

kitchen

WC

garden
where applicable

spatical proximity

access link

Fig.24:
Systematic links with the living space

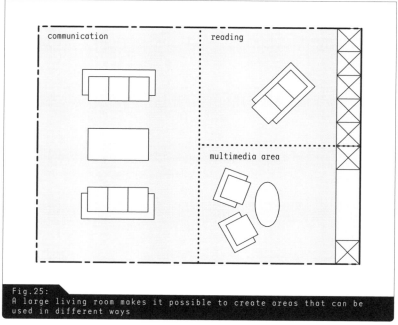

communication

reading

multimedia area

Fig.25:
A large living room makes it possible to create areas that can be
used in different ways

be defined by the occupant's personal requirements. In contrast, there are areas dedicated exclusively to recreation or special leisure activities, such as saunas and private swimming pools. Special children's play areas need possible visual links with other use areas, so that adults can keep in personal contact and supervise the children, ideally at the same time as doing other things. Open kitchen-dining rooms, living areas, and passageways offer a good opportunity in this sense: an eye can be kept on them from any adjacent area. > see chapter Elements of living, Circulation areas

> 🔖

Links with the
outdoor space

Recreation and leisure areas inside the home benefit greatly from including outdoor space. For example, ground floor apartments can build outdoor spaces into the interior concept if the weather is suitable, and thus extend the living space. > see Fig. 26 Large or small balconies and roof terraces can meet similar criteria on the upper floors. As mentioned earlier, the light and position in relation to the sun are important: it is recommended that generous apertures be created for the afternoon and evening sun, so that the living and leisure area can be naturally lit at the principal times the space is used.

HYGIENE

Uses and
functions

Physical hygiene is expressed in various forms. Whatever individual cleaning rituals may look like, they are important to life and health. Water is the central theme in hygiene, and traditionally plays a major part in many cultures. Seen entirely practically, the water has to be supplied

🔖

\\ Hint:
Little extras for children can be built into
a home without a great deal of effort. To
achieve this, an attempt can be made to see
a design for a home or a well-built house
through the eyes of a child. Small niches
become potential hiding places, the table
that folds up against the wall can become an
Indian tepee with the help of a tablecloth,
and a small corner window mysteriously lets
the sun shine on a tile pattern at a certain
time. Children are masters of design and
improvisation. Everything they need is in
their imagination and in tiny elements of room
design.

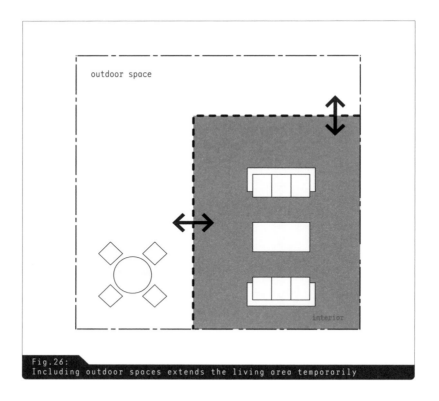

Fig.26:
Including outdoor spaces extends the living area temporarily

in a completely pure condition and disposed of after use. The necessary infrastructure makes a bathroom a very specialized function area within the home. Unlike other areas it cannot be "converted" without difficulty, and should address the needs of different users. The bathroom and guest WC need a certain among of sight and sound insulation, so as not to affect other use areas, or be affected by them.

It makes sense for bath and private WC to be placed in the immediate vicinity of the sleeping area, so that there can be direct access to them. If this is impossible, access to the bathroom, as well as to the bedroom area, should be screened from eye contact from less private areas. The cloakroom is placed in the entrance area of a home where possible, and can serve the general living areas here. › see Fig. 27

If a home ground plan is restricted in size, several functions are often grouped together in a bathroom. The WC can be in here as well as the

🖊
\\ Hint:

When planning, particularly for housing with
more than one storey, the walls in which
plumbing for fresh and sewage water are
fitted should be one above the other wherever
possible, to reduce installation difficulties
and noise pollution. Good sound insulation
should be considered at the planning stage,
especially for adjacent homes. For example,
the plumbing walls in two adjacent homes can
be next to each other and thus not affect any
other rooms. To keep the pipe runs short, the
sanitary equipment should be fixed as close to
the plumbing walls as possible.

bathtub, shower and washbasin, perhaps with bidet, baby-changing table, washing machine and tumble dryer. Bathrooms are all too commonly
rooms with minimal space and a high degree of functionalization. The
fundamental question arises of whether things have been combined here
that actually belong together. In the above example, three areas overlap:
personal hygiene, washing clothes and using the WC. Thought could be
given to whether the standard of hygiene in many ground plan solutions
in old and new buildings do justice to functions and users. If an area for
ancillary functions is planned, the laundry area could be placed elsewhere.
> see chapter Elements of living, Ancillary functions Alternatively, a washing machine
can also be placed in the kitchen, in the dressing area or in other ancillary
rooms. If use of the WC and the personal hygiene area can also be separated spatially, the bathroom can become a pleasant and clean place for
relaxation and cleansing.

Room concepts   Strict application of such standards, however, seldom produces high-
quality rooms. > see Fig. 28 The question of whether a space-saving bathroom
with shower, washbasin and toilet should be planned, or whether it is possible to design a generous bathroom with a generous amount of space depends above all on the area available.

In order to create functional focal points, dividing elements, for example, can be installed in the bathroom to separate off special areas and
also increase efficiency. > see Fig. 29 A compact personal hygiene area can be
created with shower and washbasin, with a separate area for the bathtub.
The toilet and the bidet, if fitted, are also separated off in the bathroom or

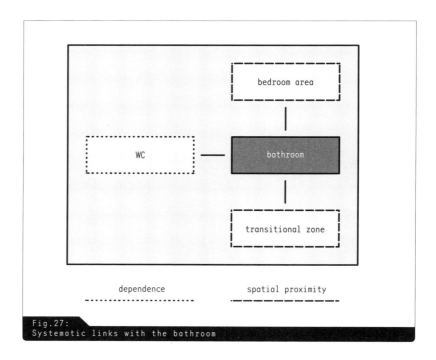

allotted a rooms of their own. An arrangement of this kind can avoid block-
ages and unpleasant odours, especially in the morning. In larger house-
holds an additional WC (cloakroom) makes sense anyway.

Apart from its functional aspects, the bathroom can be seen as a
place where it is pleasant to spend time. For example, it is possible to
move away from the usual washbasin, bath and shower pattern and look
for special ground plan and function solutions. A shower base can be replaced by a custom-sized area with a floor-level drain. Or a (large) bath-

\\ Hint:
Architectural visions for innovative and
forward-looking bathrooms can be found in
Bathroom Unplugged by Dirk Hebel and Jörg
Stollmann (eds.), Birkhäuser Publishers,
Basel 2005.

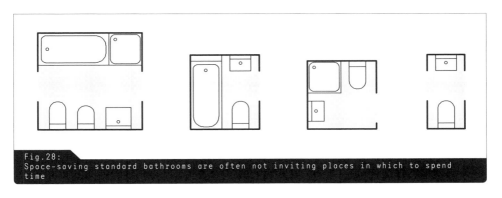

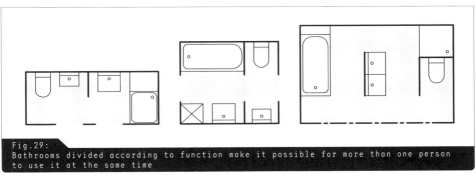

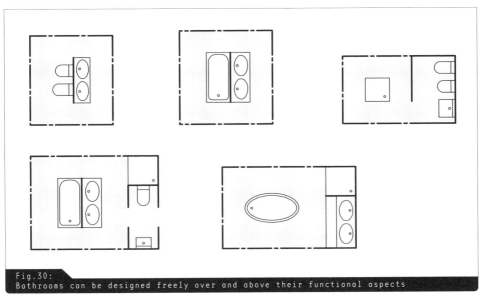

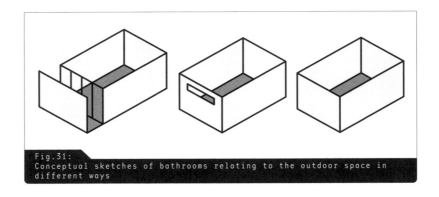

Fig.31:
Conceptual sketches of bathrooms relating to the outdoor space in different ways

tub is arranged standing free in the middle of the room, giving a sense of spaciousness and the extra room for moving about. Such solutions may well need more space, but enhance the quality of living in the bathroom function area. > see Fig. 30

Links with the outside area

Even though the bathroom is a very intimate area, its relationship with the outdoor space should not be neglected. If this outside area is not overlooked, a large area of glass or a small balcony can be very attractive. Cleverly chosen window apertures can create visual links with the outdoor space, without impairing the intimacy of the interior.

Bathrooms placed away from the outside walls do not allow any visual contact with the outside world or permit natural ventilation, and so have to be ventilated mechanically. On grounds of ventilation problems alone, windowless bathrooms are not as attractive to spend time in as baths with windows in the outside wall. One interesting variant for a bathroom without outside walls could be a glazed opening in the roof. This can take account of functional aspects of lighting and ventilation, and also gives a clear view of the sky from the bathtub. > see Fig. 31 right

COOKING

Uses and functions

Cooking has lost its vital importance in recent decades. It is no longer necessary for individuals to cook in order to eat. Fast food and ready meals determine a great deal of the menu for many Western people, and mass production means that the food industry can offer rock-bottom prices for tinned and frozen products. But cooking can be about more than preparing food in a way that is as time-saving as possible. It can be a communal activity, carry a high level of leisure value and not least promote awareness of knowing what we eat.

As a rule the kitchen is a busy part of the home, and is thus of crucial importance. For example, it should not be too far away from the home's entrance so that food purchases do not have to be carried too far. Storage areas and vegetable gardens, where applicable, also need to be close to the kitchen. The eating area is served from the kitchen, and should be directly accessible, so that food can be put on the table and dirty dishes removed without undue difficulty. › see Fig. 32

Room concepts The kitchen can be defined in very different ways within a room concept. It can take up the space appropriate to a cooking niche, working kitchen or kitchen-dining room in its various forms, according to need and aspirations. If it is treated as an isolated functional unit it will be given a room of its own, clearly separated from other use areas. This room can perform its function through optimized areas and be merely a working area in which to cook. But it can also be made into an attractive place to spend time in and, for example, set up a snack area or a full eating area in a kitchen and thus create a central meeting place in the home. › see chapter Elements of living, Eating Alternatively, people often like to plan open kitchens, which will then merge into other use areas. › see

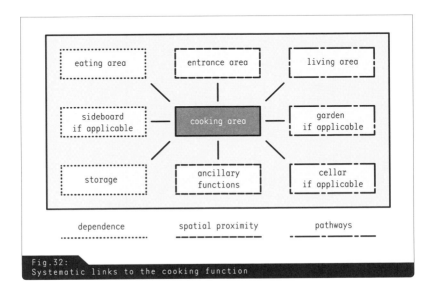

Fig.32:
Systematic links to the cooking function

In this way, cooking as an activity is in communication with other living areas, and benefits from an integrated spatial concept. However, it should be noted that the open situation means that the cooking smells will affect the area for some time. In order to handle functional and spatial aspects flexibly, large (sliding) doors can provide temporary separation.

Links with outdoor space

Links with the space outside are essential for the kitchen, and not only for reasons of light and ventilation. If the kitchen is used frequently, by a family with children, for example, it is advantageous to be able to watch the children playing outside. In good weather, an attached terrace or balcony can be attractive for breakfast or another light meal.

Furnishings

The kitchen is divided up by work surfaces, cooker, sideboard, and sink with draining board. These working areas can be arranged in different combinations. Short distances to walk and fluent work sequences, combined with sufficient area to move around in, allow a high degree of functionality. Typical arrangements, depending on the area available, are kitchens with one or two runs of furniture, or U-shaped or L-shaped kitchens. › see Fig. 33

As well as this, free arrangements and central placing of cooker and worktops can be selected; these make the kitchen into a place with special qualities in terms of its function and style. › see Fig. 34 If a kitchen block is freestanding, it makes it easier to communicate with other areas or people, as users are not looking at a wall while working.

The kitchen is a functional place, a workplace within the home. Food should be easily accessible and often has to be stored in cool conditions. If utensils such as pots, pans and knives are well arranged and stored so that they can be seen clearly, this makes the individual working stages easier.

› see chapter Elements of living, Storage

\\ Tip:
Ventilation is a key topic for kitchens, as cooking can produce very intrusive smells. For this reason, effective natural or mechanical ventilation should be provided.

\\ Hint:
Forward-looking kitchen concepts of recent decades, planning fundamentals and current trends are presented in detail in *The Kitchen* by Klaus Spechtenhauser (ed.), Birkhäuser Publishers, Basel 2006.

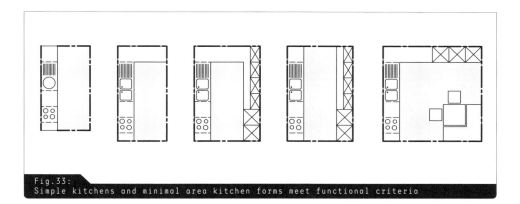

Fig.33:
Simple kitchens and minimal area kitchen forms meet functional criteria

\\ Hint:
Generally, the depth of the movement area in
front of kitchen furniture should not be less
than 1.2 m, as otherwise people could get in
each other's way. Worktops must be at least
90 cm high and adjustable above the plinth to
match the users' height. The standard depth of
kitchen cupboards under worktops, and fixed
elements such as cooker and refrigerator, is
60 cm, thus giving the usual depth for a run of
furniture.

\\ Tip:
Windows above the worktop permit visual
contact with the outside world when working.
But it is often difficult to adjust the sill
height of such windows to the other windows
when seen from the outside, as the height
of the kitchen furniture means windows
above worktops in a kitchen have to be
correspondingly higher. If opening windows are
placed behind a sink, the fitted height of the
taps must also be considered, as otherwise it
may be impossible to open the window.

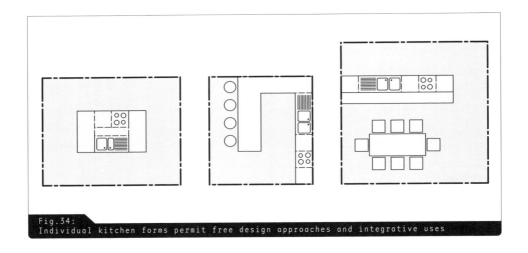

ANCILLARY FUNCTIONS

Uses and
functions

Ancillary functions include washing, drying and ironing clothes. A special room is not needed for this, and other areas can be used temporarily to perform these tasks. But if it is possible to build a utility room for ancillary functions into the home programme, these activities can be combined sensibly. Like the kitchen and the bathroom, this room is a functional space earmarked for a particular purpose. For example, it can provide space for washing machine and dryer or washing lines. Here, laundry can be ironed and stored, along with household equipment and cleaning materials. A separate shower can do good service as well, so that it is possible to clean up when coming in from outdoors without impinging on more sensitive areas of the home. If the utility room is in a functional area together with the kitchen, they can be used at the same time and the distances travelled will be shorter. Depending on the overall concept, it can also make sense to place them near the bathrooms and bedrooms, where laundry is usually generated, and this avoids walking long distances to the washing machine.

STORAGE

Uses and
functions

People need a large number of objects in the course of a normal day. We surround ourselves with functional objects and personal memorabilia. Some of them are intended for daily use, and are well organized and stored functionally, while others have a special significance and are intended to be seen. A home is often a motley collection of a whole variety of objects and also a kind of personal museum that reflects the occupant's personality.

Storage
categories

We can distinguish between various storage categories. A private library imposes order on books while making them into exhibits; a collection of CDs or records makes it possible to play the desired music and not least expresses the owner's personal taste. These display forms of storage often have in common that they display personally important objects. A different approach is generally taken to everyday items such as clothing, shoes, kitchen utensils, cleaning equipment and comparable objects. They should usually be easily accessible, protected from dirt, and ideally invisible. They therefore tend to be arranged according to functional criteria and put away temporarily. Finally, a home also needs areas where things that are not in constant use can be stored efficiently over the long term. These will be objects that are seldom needed or are used seasonally, which would tend to be a nuisance elsewhere. In the field of tension between functionality and aesthetics, considerable significance is accorded to the places that display, organize and arrange things from various points of view.

> 🗓

Room concepts

Beautiful and valuable objects, or those that are significant in some other way, affect and lend form to a room. Well-lit and proportioned areas of wall for pictures can be just as much of a design characteristic of a home as an open, room-dividing shelf system. An indentation in the floor covered with plate glass that can be walked on, or visual links with display niches and central gaps in walls, are all ways of presenting things in a home. It is also possible to create special rooms for collectors' items, or to use transit spaces as a gallery or library. > see chapter **Elements of living, Circulation areas** You do not have to be an art collector to know how to make

🗓
\\ Hint:
As a rule of thumb, at least 2 percent of the
overall space available in the home should be
set aside for separate storage.

good use of this kind of design approach: it can appeal to many people who have things with which they like to surround themselves. In this context, quantity does not necessarily enhance the quality of a home, as living space can also acquire its characteristics from a few elements, which then make more of an impact.

Storing everyday objects Objects that are put away temporarily and used often require functional storage space. Small spaces for storing cleaning materials or food should be planned in relation to the areas in which these objects will often be used.

Cupboards, chests of drawers and shelves can be fitted in a kitchen or bedroom as needed, and in an appropriate style. › see chapter Elements of living, Sleeping, and Cooking

Long-term storage Storage space for the long term can be created in special spaces, in the cellar or attic if necessary. Spaces in the loft and under the stairs can also be allotted a function and activated, as can niches and corners. Good accessibility and efficiency are important. In the case of storage rooms that are not used very often, care should be taken to provide adequate ventilation where necessary, to avoid damp or stale air.

CIRCULATION AREAS

Uses and functions The indoor circulation areas in a home provide access to the areas dedicated to different uses. They separate and provide buffer zones between areas, but at the same time they connect them, and determine the routes taken through the home. They convey impressions of space, and their situation and volume greatly influence the quality of living. They need space, and just like all the other spaces in a home they need to relate correctly to building costs and designated uses.

Entrance areas in a home The hall is the entrance area to a home, and precedes all the other rooms. › see Fig. 35

In apartments, a hall is necessary for sound insulation purposes; it can also have some sort of climatic protection for the door. Natural lighting and the relationship between the area and height of rooms are significant here. › see chapter Basics, Creating space As the entrance area, a hall creates a transition from inside to outside, and provides a place where outdoor clothing can be left and guests received. According to the individual approach, it can be a minimal buffer zone or become an imposing entrance to the home. Without this important intermediate area, other use areas

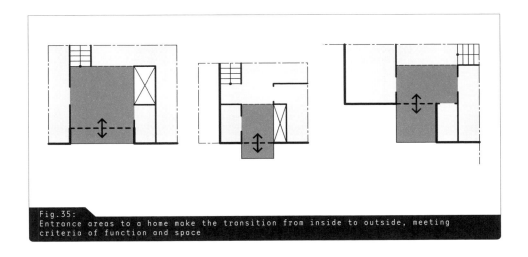

Fig.35:
Entrance areas to a home make the transition from inside to outside, meeting criteria of function and space

may be disturbed or hampered. For example, the hall often provides direct access to the public living area, the kitchen, the cloakroom and the area where outdoor clothing is stored. In addition, it commonly also serves as a distribution area to other parts of the home and borders internal stairs and corridors.

Internal corridors

In hierarchically arranged homes, the corridors enable movement between areas used in different ways. If a corridor is not on the periphery of the home, and not naturally lit, it is an unattractive place in which to spend time: long, dark corridors have an unpleasant effect, and can generally be avoided by a clever overall design. Open ground plans make it broadly possible to manage without internal corridors, as the different areas merge into each other seamlessly. › see chapter Basics, Creating space

Transit spaces

If a corridor is naturally lit and covers a reasonably large area, its spatial quality is enhanced and it can serve as a temporary area in which to play and spend time, beyond its basic function. › see Fig. 36

Trapped spaces

Spaces accessed from a transitional area are called "trapped spaces" as they have no access structure of their own. Parts of a large room can also be portioned off with light, fitted structures (cupboards, screens or similar), so that the zone behind them can be used as a private circulation area. Seen in this way, an open ground plan consists of many transit areas, as the different zones run directly into each other and fuse with the access areas. › see chapter Basics, Creating space

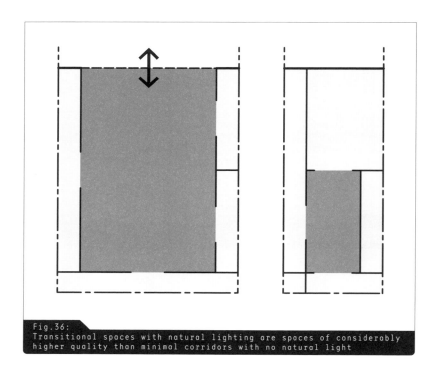

Fig.36:
Transitional spaces with natural lighting are spaces of considerably higher quality than minimal corridors with no natural light

Stairs

If a residential unit has more than one floor, stairs are needed. These stairs can be open plan, in another space such as the hall or living room, thus emphasizing the transition to the next level. Alternatively, it can be in a space of its own, screening off the upper floor. It must comply with functional and design principles, and those stipulated in building regulations. > see Fig. 37

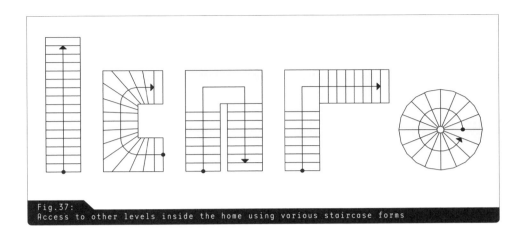

BUILDING FORMS

The previous chapters dealt with the subject of homes mainly from the perspective of space and use. This chapter will categorize dwellings in terms of typologically different forms, the specific qualities of which affect living concepts considerably.

DETACHED AND SEMI-DETACHED HOUSES

Detached houses

Detached houses provide accommodation for a single family. They need to be a prescribed distance away from neighbouring buildings, according to local building regulations, and often require a considerable amount of space for garden and infrastructure. In comparison with an urban structure, these areas accumulate to reduce housing density. › see Fig. 38

Implications
for occupants

Fundamentally, a detached house makes individual, and above all independent, living possible. Stylistic and other requirements can be interpreted on a personal scale in the design; there is a great deal of creative

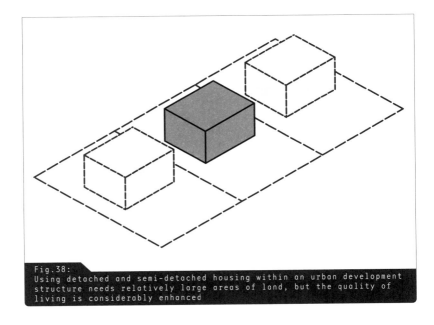

Fig. 38:
Using detached and semi-detached housing within an urban development structure needs relatively large areas of land, but the quality of living is considerably enhanced

> ⓘ

scope. These individual ideas, and the inclusion of a private outdoor space in the form of garden use, permit a wide range of design approaches.

Living on two
levels

Single-family houses often involve living on two levels: the entrance floor commonly combines areas for general use like the kitchen, dining and living rooms. Areas for essentially private use such as hygiene and sleeping are then placed on the upper floor. But additional levels can also structure the space sensibly, according to need and the finance available. > see chapter Basics, Zoning, and Creating space

Bungalows

In bungalows, the use areas are arranged on a single level. Their low height means they may fit in very well in a country setting. The building is zoned within its own area, and can derive three-dimensional impact from projections and recesses, and create links with local features.

Semi-detached
houses

Semi-detached houses combine two homes, each for one family, within a single building, and reduce construction costs by cutting down outside spaces. > see Fig. 39 The ground plans are often in mirror image from the middle, and vary only minimally, but it is possible in principle to build two different houses under the same roof. Changes of shape and material can be matched to each other, and convey a uniform impression despite different design approaches.

Terraced houses

Terraces are created by designing a row of uniform houses with identical ground plans or by accumulating individual built units. They are often conceived to save space, and are thus an economical way of building. They commonly occupy very little land, and restrict the width of the plot to the width of one house. > see Fig. 40

Such houses can be built in various ways: the fronts of the houses can be in a straight line, a circle or on the diagonal, and they can be arranged

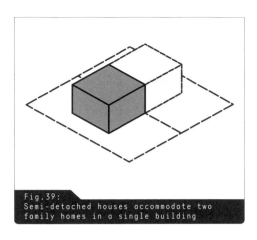

Fig.39:
Semi-detached houses accommodate two
family homes in a single building

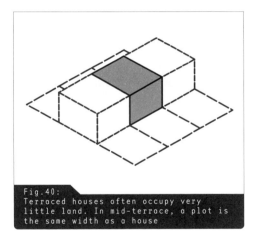

Fig.40:
Terraced houses often occupy very
little land. In mid-terrace, a plot is
the same width as a house

in rows or around the periphery of a block. Building terraced houses produces a high urban density that relates to a high quality of living and the much-propagated development approach of a structured and yet not unduly tight urban format.

Implications
for occupants   The lighting possibilities are restricted in comparison with detached and semi-detached houses: except in the first and last houses in a terrace, the front and rear façades afford only two sources of natural light. For this

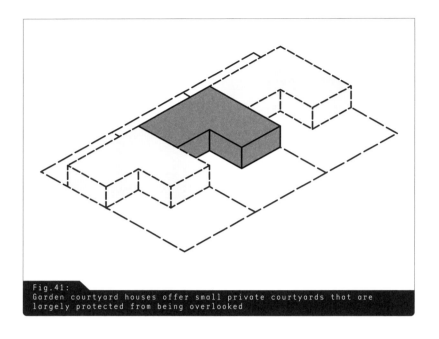

reason the orientation of the various rooms for particular purposes must be matched up very carefully. > see chapter Basics, Orientation Although terracing limits individual aspects of the outside space, independent approaches can emerge.

Garden courtyard houses

Garden courtyard houses are a particular form of terracing. Small private courtyards are formed using the end of the house next door, and these are largely protected from being overlooked. > see Fig. 41 This central outdoor space provides a meeting place for all the rooms facing it. As all the windows in the rear section look onto the courtyard, there may be a problem in creating areas for private retreat.

"Chain" terraces

To break up the visual impact of the façade, the houses are often staggered or made into chains by projecting or being recessed evenly. > see Fig. 42

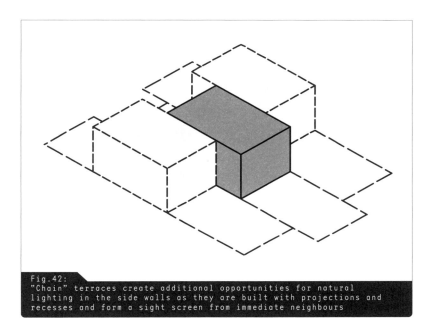

MULTI-STOREY HOUSING

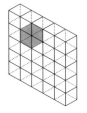

Unlike single-family houses, multi-storey housing combines several residential units in a complex building, arranged adjacent to or above each other on several floors. Developing multiple levels on a relatively small amount of land increases urban density.

Block periphery
development

Block periphery development is a closed construction form. A single building, or a series of individual buildings, encloses an inner courtyard and thus creates an interior area that is different from the outside. (see Fig. 43) A block periphery development can be constructed in a variety of shapes. Rectangular developments are just as acceptable as circular and curved structures, mixed forms or other geometrical figures. According to its size and shape, the enclosed inner area can be structured by other buildings and divided into additional courtyards. Inner courtyards permit all kinds of design approaches and opportunities for use. Possible access to the outside world through gates, passages and entrances offer public, semi-public and private use. Green spaces, designs such as urban squares,

> 🔎

garden zones and play areas are conceivable, and so are cafés, shops and small public parks.

Implications
for occupants

If the internal area is largely sheltered from the outside world, it is also protected, in an urban setting in particular, from external influences such as noise, exhaust fumes and being overlooked. This inner area is often semi-public in character, and is appropriately designed to provide the occupants with green and play areas as a place for retreat. Living rooms and bedrooms can face this quiet interior space, entrance and ancillary rooms front the urban outside where possible, and form an internal buffer against being overlooked and noise. But an urban block can also simply frame an inner area, which then becomes a public sphere by means of a raised ground floor, passageways and other openings, and is able to invite urban life into it.

Building in rows

This structures a series of individual buildings or uniform blocks in rows. > see Fig. 44 Although this could not be simpler as a basic form, the way the various rows are placed in relation to each other can create a variety of urban arrangements. Parallel, right-angled or diagonal arrangements may be considered. Differentiated lengths and heights can create or adopt spatial links within a complex structure. Building in rows does not separate inside and outside areas from each other as clearly as block periphery development. If the rows are arranged entirely in parallel, the gaps created are open at the ends. This affords good opportunities for natural lighting and ventilation, but the development can be affected by noise, dust and wind, especially in large complexes spread over a wide area. In addition, the spaces in between have little inherent quality, as they are framed on two sides only and are often subject to intense visual control over the length of an entire row. One possible alternative is to close the open ends

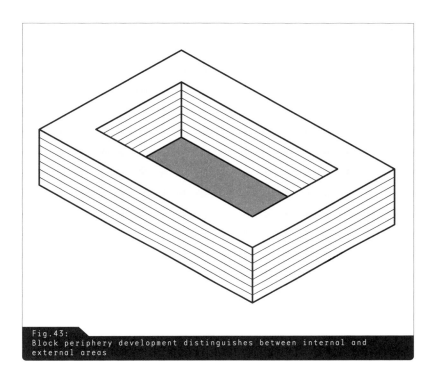

of a series of rows with more rows of buildings arranged at right angles. This creates internal areas that seem more closed in spatial terms and create semi-public, calmed areas.

Implications
for occupants

Rows can be arranged in a clear east-west or north-south pattern, so that the areas devoted to various uses function well. › see chapter Basics, Orientation Unlike a closed block, no special solutions are needed for corners, which must be adapted to deal with particular aspects of access, natural light and ventilation. This means that standard ground plans can easily be implemented.

Block and row developments are usually characterized by coherent measures that put their stamp on a large area as urban development conceptions.

Solitaire
buildings

In contrast, solitaire multi-storey buildings are usually planned with greater distances between the individual buildings, and it is quite common

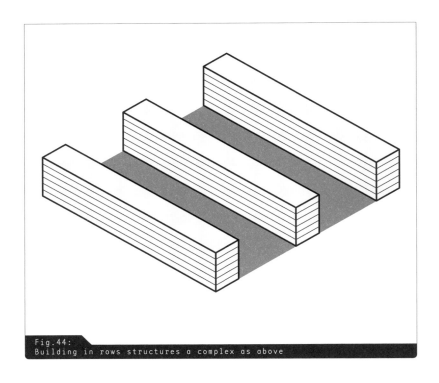

for them to be higher and longer. Such large dimensions can mean that a group of solitaire buildings do not produce coherent, spatially differentiated intermediate areas on a human scale.

Slab blocks

Slab blocks have a linear structure with a compact construction form that often reaches considerable heights and lengths. › see Fig. 45 left If combined into a communal complex, it is scarcely possible even for several slab blocks to create internal areas, so they often generate large intermediate areas that are not so simple to design.

Large forms

Slab blocks can be combined to create large forms, and as such can be planned individually or lend character to a large-scale development. › see Fig. 45 centre It is not impossible to differentiate space through a creative basic form and grouping, but it can be applied only to a limited extent because the areas involved are so large.

Point building development

Point building developments are made up of solitaire buildings placed freely within the surrounding area. › see Fig. 45 right Appropriate design of their contours can impose three-dimensional form on the buildings and thus underline their vertical quality. The undirected ground plan forms mean that the individual buildings have little relationship with the space around them, and because they are necessarily so far apart, it is impossible to create differentiated spaces in between even when they are placed in groups.

Implications
for the
occupants

> ρ

Solitaire building forms bring a large number of residential units together in one high-rise construction. Optimizing the ground and circulation areas makes it possible to create compact and complex housing structures that organize living space for large numbers of people within a relatively small area.

The living areas can be realized in a fundamentally individual way, or in a standardized form. But for economic reasons large-scale building schemes are usually realized uniformly, with standard ground plans that can be executed as various different types if need be, so that different dwelling concepts can be offered. General access structures restrict the development of individualized units, and emphasize the communal character of the building. The use of gardens linked directly to an individual home is possible only for ground floor apartments. Large or small balconies and roof terraces also create private outdoor space in multi-storey blocks. Extensive views of the surrounding area can be an advantage on the higher

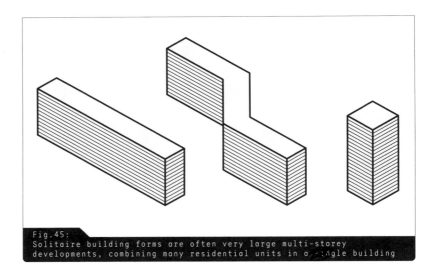

Fig.45:
Solitaire building forms are often very large multi-storey
developments, combining many residential units in a single building

floors. But the homes are exposed to particular weather conditions accord-ing to the level on which they are placed. High-rise dwellings can enjoy natural ventilation only to a limited extent because of their considerable height and strong winds.

\\ Hint:
Access is regulated by stairs, combinations of
stairs, and lifts and emergency staircases,
according to the height of the building
and the appropriate regulations. A lift
should be included for buildings of more
than four storeys, as the individual units
cannot otherwise be accessed suitably. High-
rise provisions within the local building
regulations stipulate the access and fire
protection requirements. These should be
addressed before drawing up a final design,
and they often have a far-reaching impact on
the way access and space is structured.

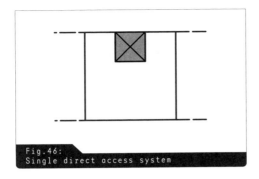

Fig.46:
Single direct access system

ACCESS

Solitaires and rows of detached and semi-detached houses all have their own internal access structures and independent entrances. This makes it possible to establish a sense of a personal address, and the individual use of these dwelling and construction forms is emphasized. Private access of this kind can also be implemented in principle in multi-storey homes, but generally means elaborate staircase structures are needed. Access systems for multi-storey apartment blocks are introduced systematically below. They bring general access areas such as building entrances, stairs and lifts together centrally and communally.

A typology can be established for various access forms. We distinguish between blocks with direct staircase access and blocks with corridor access. Both types are possible in principle for multi-storey blocks, according to the building form. However, corridor access makes economic sense only for projects involving considerable building length and uniform access systems.

Direct staircase access types

Blocks with direct staircase access allot a certain number of residential units to a central access area. The more homes per floor are accessed, the more economically the whole block can be built, as more occupants share an access point and there is a good relationship of circulation space to usable space.

Single direct access

Single access blocks provide access to one home per floor, and are essentially an uneconomical form, because a communal staircase provides access to only a limited number of homes and the costs fall to a small number of residential units. › see Fig. 46 It is usual to restrict such blocks to four storeys, so that no lift is needed. Advantages accrue from the freely

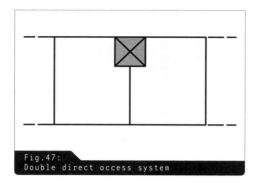

Fig.47:
Double direct access system

available lighting and ventilation possibilities, and in the design of the ground plans, as no constraints are imposed by other units on each floor.

Double direct access

Double direct access blocks provide access to two homes per floor and thus improve the ratio of access needs to use. › see Fig. 47 For rational construction the ground plans are often in mirror image on a central axis, but it is possible to realize different units in terms of room division and size. Advantages include the possibility of lateral ventilation from one side of the building to the other, and natural lighting on at least two sides, which permits the use areas to be favourably oriented.

›

Triple direct access

Triple direct access blocks provide access to three homes per floor. › see Fig. 48 Different dwelling sizes and plans take account of different user needs, and can thus enable a greater mixture of user profiles in a block. Depending on how the units are divided up, it can result in the ground plans facing one way, which creates constraints in orienting the different

\\ Hint:
Single and double direct access systems
can be readily supplied with fresh air by
lateral ventilation. This means a home can be
ventilated from one side of the building to
another, and thus all the air in a dwelling
is replaced in a short ventilation period.
A brief spell of intensive ventilation
guarantees a complete change of air and heat
loss is kept to a minimum.

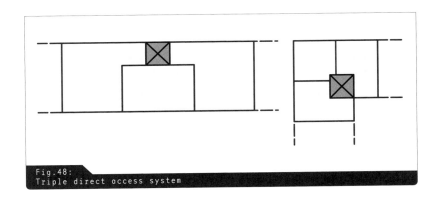

Fig.48:
Triple direct access system

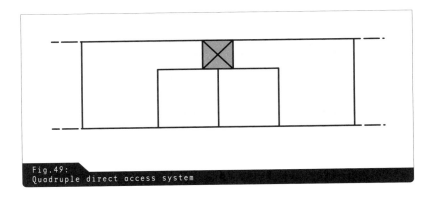

Fig.49:
Quadruple direct access system

use areas. The possibility of lateral ventilation is also limited. Triple direct access is particularly suitable for ground plans in the corners of the buildings.

Quadruple
direct access

Quadruple direct access allows simultaneous access to four dwellings on one level and is therefore an economical form. › see Fig. 49 The range of unit sizes and versions can be varied very considerably. Large and small units can be built on every floor. As in triple direct access, it can lead to single-sided orientation and restrictions on lateral ventilation.

Point blocks

As solitaire construction forms, point blocks cannot be arranged in series like direct staircase access types. They group the residential units by floor around a central, vertical access core. The number and size of the units are based on the floor area of the structure. In principle, units can face in two directions, which then offers opportunities for reasonable

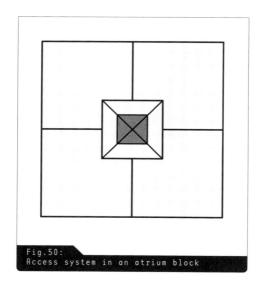

natural lighting and ventilation conditions – but only with up to four units per floor.

Atrium
buildings

Atrium buildings represent a particular form of point block in multi-storey construction. › see Fig. 50 Here, a light well admits natural light to the centre of the building, restricting its height, as sunlight can reach the lower floors to a limited extent only. An atrium makes it possible to avoid dark and unattractive access areas inside the building, and also creates semi-private zones in front of units, giving an impression of lavish space.

Corridor types

Residential blocks with corridors have vertical access that serves corridor systems, which in turn provide horizontal access to a certain number of adjacent residential units.

The vertical access areas can be placed centrally or structured sectionally, according to the length of the building. If the corridor is inside the building, it is known as an internal corridor, if it is outside, it is an external, or open corridor (covered walkway).

Internal
corridor

An internal corridor provides efficient access, as the outer skin of the building can then be used completely for lighting and ventilating the residential units. › see Fig. 51 Conversely, an internal corridor receives very

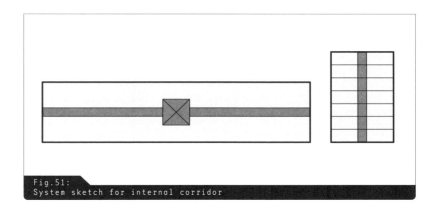

Fig. 51:
System sketch for internal corridor

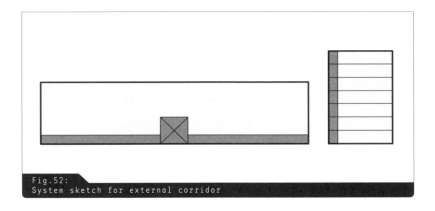

Fig. 52:
System sketch for external corridor

little natural light. This means that such corridors are often dark and long, are uncomfortable to be in and tend to carry unpleasant associations. To avoid access situations of this kind, semi-public spaces can be created at reasonable intervals along the corridor. They break through to the outer façade and thus admit natural light to the middle of the floor. Such spaces accommodate vertical access cores like stairs and lifts, or are designed as waiting areas and meeting-points.

External corridor / covered walkway

Because they are placed on the outer wall of the building, external corridors have no lighting problems and can also be organized to be open on the outside, i.e. without glass or other separating structures. › see Fig. 52 However, there are climatic considerations, especially for tall buildings.

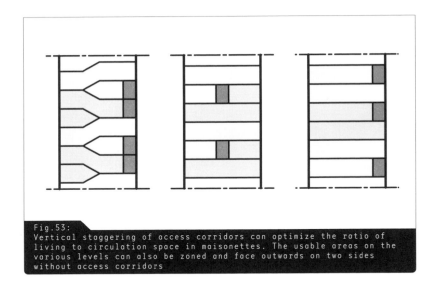

Fig.53:
Vertical staggering of access corridors can optimize the ratio of living to circulation space in maisonettes. The usable areas on the various levels can also be zoned and face outwards on two sides without access corridors

Wind and the risk of ice formation restrict the function of a covered walkway.

Vertical
staggering
Essentially, every floor can have internal or external corridors. But an arrangement of this kind can mean ground plans are one-sided, as the corridors screen direct access to the outside of the building on one side, and even where they are external, only subordinate use areas can be placed on the corridor side. In a case like this, apartments and studio flats may be an attractive solution. If the homes are also connected vertically inside the building as maisonettes, access corridors are needed only every second or third floor, in internal or external corridor systems. › see Fig. 53, and chapter Basics, Creating space So for one thing the ratio of living to access space is optimized, and for another, lateral ventilation is possible through the full depth of the building, and the usable areas can face the outside on two sides on at least one floor. Of course maisonettes are not restricted to corridor access blocks alone. Direct stair access types and mixed forms can benefit from splitting a dwelling over several levels. Creating maisonettes is a good way of making two small residential units into one big one, particularly in old buildings, thus taking account of present-day requirements and needs.

IN CONCLUSION

"Building means designing life processes."

Walter Gropius

As an architectural discipline, housing construction offers almost unlimited creative possibilities. Designing key life processes can be associated with modern techniques and materials and a high level of comfort and style. The primal nature of the basic needs that are satisfied by creating living space can stimulate people to concentrate on essentials in a rapid and highly technological world. Housing construction intentions and methods have undergone considerable change in the course of history, but the most important parameter, the human being, has changed very little. It is still about creating appropriate, human living space that is capable of facing the future. New approaches and open thinking enjoy a similar status to looking back at the history of housing. Numerous ideas, insights and tried-and-tested concepts can be combined with fresh ideas, up-to-date forms of expression and new techniques. At present, housing quality is particularly associated with aspects of ecology and energy. In addition, demographic changes in our society are increasingly making an impact, and demanding appropriate housing. The benchmark for every potential solution in response to these challenges should be human beings and their basic needs, if the future is to be designed meaningfully. It is a matter not just of meeting the necessary housing requirements, but also of creating quality of life and accommodation, and continuing to question familiar and standardized housing typologies – above all, to create an environment that does not prescribe people's way of life, but in which they can develop creatively and design their individual ways of living together.

APPENDIX

LITERATURE

Andrea Deplazes (ed.): *Constructing Architecture*, Birkhäuser Publishers, Basel 2005

Klaus-Peter Gast: *Living Plans*, Birkhäuser Publishers, Basel 2005

Manuel Gausa, Jaime Salazar: *Housing / Single Family Housing*, Birkhäuser Publishers, Basel 2002

Dirk Hebel, Jörg Stollmann (eds.): *Bathroom Unplugged*, Birkhäuser Publishers, Basel 2005

Ernst Neufert, Peter Neufert: *Architects' Data*, 3rd edition, Blackwell Science, UK USA Australia 2004

Périphériques / IN-EX projects: *Your House Now*, Birkhäuser Publishers, Basel 2003

Friederike Schneider (ed.): *Floor Plan Manual*, Birkhäuser Publishers, Basel 2004

Camillo Sitte: *The Birth of Modern City Planning: With a translation of the 1889 Austrian edition of his City Planning According to Artistic Principles*, Dover Publications, USA 2006

Klaus Spechtenhauser (ed.): *The Kitchen*, Birkhäuser Publishers, Basel 2005

Marcus Vitruvius Pollio: *Vitruvius: The Ten Books on Architecture*, Cambridge University Press, Cambridge UK 2001

Series editor: Bert Bielefeld
Conception: Bert Bielefeld, Annette Gref

Layout and Cover design: Muriel Comby
Translation into English: Michael Robinson
English Copy editing: Monica Buckland

Figures page 8, 28, 54 Bert Bielefeld, all other
illustrations by the author.
Quotation page 71: Systematische Vorarbeit für
rationellen Wohnungsbau. In: magazine "bauhaus"
1. Jhg. Nr. 2, Dessau 1927

A CIP catalogue record for this book is available
from the Library of Congress, Washington D.C.,
USA

Bibliographic information published by
Die Deutsche Bibliothek
Die Deutsche Bibliothek lists this publication
in the Deutsche Nationalbibliografie; detailed
bibliographic data is available on the Internet at
http://dnb.ddb.de.

This book is also available in a German (ISBN 3-
7643-7646-5) and a French (ISBN 3-7643-7953-7)
language edition.

© 2007 Birkhäuser –Publishers for Architecture,
P.O. Box 133, CH-4010 Basel, Switzerland
Member of Springer Science + Business Media

Printed on acid-free paper produced from
chlorine-free pulp. TCF ∞
Printed in Germany

ISBN-10: 3-7643-7647-3
ISBN-13: 978-3-7643-7647-5

9 8 7 6 5 4 3 2 1   www.birkhauser.ch